GW00890272

Leave It in
the Hands of
a Specialist

Jesse Duplantis

JDM Publications

Leave It in the Hands of a Specialist
ISBN 978-0-9728712-6-6
Copyright © 1993
by Jesse Duplantis

10th Printing - June 2011
Published by Jesse Duplantis Ministries
PO Box 1089
Destrehan, Louisiana 70047
USA
www.jdm.org

Jesse Duplantis Ministries is dedicated to reaching people and changing lives with the Gospel of Jesus Christ. For more information, or to purchase other products from Jesse Duplantis Ministries, please contact us at the address above.

Leave it in the Hands of a Specialist

Down in South Louisiana, we eat something that people all around the world wince in disgust at the thought of eating - *crawfish*. Man, we love them! When crawfish season begins in the spring, we boil them by the pound in giant pots filled with spicy crab boil seasoning, cloves of garlic, hot sausage, potatoes and little, short cobs of corn.

Then, we pour thousands of them onto long tables while they're still steaming hot, start pinching the tails from the heads and just enjoy ourselves. It's a cultural thing, and unless you're from here, you probably just don't get it.

Because I travel a lot, I meet many people who want to know about my culture, and they especially want to know why we eat crawfish.

"How can you eat those ugly things?!" they ask in disgust.

"The same way you eat yours," I say, "A cow ain't exactly the prettiest thing I've ever seen, and hogs don't look that good to me either. I've never seen a big hog and thought it looked good enough to take a bite out of." They usually nod but they sure don't agree!

I find that most people aren't really

bothered by the actual crawfish meat. What really freaks them out is the *way* we serve it. They remember the photos and the television footage of us sitting at long tables while piles of bright, red, boiled crawfish are poured from giant metal pots directly onto the tables. They think it's just so uncouth.

"You just pour them all over a table," they ask, "and eat them just like that?"

"Yeah, just like that," I say. "I like them so much, I suck the juice out of the head till the eyes click!" It's not very appealing to hear about, but I guess it's the reason most Cajuns aren't skinny. With the right preparation and seasoning, there aren't too many things in this world that we can't make taste good!

Today, the Cajun culture is known around the world, and I've had many dishes outside the region that claim to be authentic. Pastors and friends have put on crawfish boils for me and tried everything they know to do to make them taste right, but I've come to believe that some things are just better off left in the hands of a specialist! Cajuns know how to handle crawfish.

Jesus Knows How to Handle People

When it comes to people, there is only one man who can handle the sin, sickness, brokenness and general misery of mankind and His name is **Jesus Christ**. He is a specialist at helping the lost find their way in life. He specializes in helping the sick, sad and broken find health, joy and wholeness through a relationship with God.

You know, most people would never check into a hospital and then refuse to follow the instructions of the doctor specializing in their illness. When a person is sick, they'll do just about anything their specialist says to be made well. It makes pretty good sense. After all, their recovery depends on the specialist's valuable instructions. Yet, many people ignore the instruction of "The Specialist," Jesus Christ.

God sent His Son into this world to give us life - an abundant life that is filled with His love, joy and peace. Jesus taught us through both His Word and His example that He was interested in helping people. He was drawn to those who were lost, sick and hurting. He didn't care if the hurting person was very poor or very rich, He reached out His hand to help them, offering words of truth to set them free.

For centuries, the Church has not really understood the ministry of Jesus. They've tried to clean people up before presenting them to God, but Jesus never taught anybody to do that - not through His words or through His own actions. Whether people were sick, lame, broke or hungry, Jesus took them just the way they were. He didn't make them jump through hoops, change their hairstyle or start acting like a "good person." He went right to the heart of matters because He knew that a changed heart was necessary for a changed life.

Today, I want to tell you that no matter where you are in life or what condition your heart is in, Jesus wants to take you in. His arms are open wide, and He specializes in every problem you can think of or get yourself into - no matter how bad!

You can't mess up enough for Jesus not to be able to help you. He's a specialist at turning around impossible situations and cleaning the hearts of people who've done more wrong than they care to tell.

If you're in need of help, Jesus is waiting for you to turn to Him - to give your life to Him and to trust Him enough to leave those problems in His capable hands.

When you leave your problems in the hands of The Specialist, you can be sure that He will cleanse your heart of sin. If you are hungry for His presence, He will satisfy your heart and meet you right where you are. Jesus went to the cross to die for your sin, and He has already paid the price for all your wrongs. So, whatever you ask forgiveness for, He will be faithful to forgive. Isaiah 53:5 says, *"But He was wounded for our transgressions, He was bruised for our iniquities: the chastisement of our peace was upon Him; and with His stripes we are healed."*

He took those stripes across His back for your healing too, and so if you're sick today, you can cry out to Him and draw on His healing power. He is a faithful God who still heals. His power is just as real and accessible today as it was two thousand years ago, because of the power of His work at the cross. Hebrews 13:8 assures of this when it says, *"Jesus Christ the same yesterday, and today, and forever."*

Do not worry. If you are burdened by the problems of life, you have a place to go in Jesus. He will never leave you nor forsake you - He is your helper, and there is nothing to fear with Him (Hebrews 13:5-6). If you'll trust Him and turn the worry of those problems over to Him, He will be faithful to deliver you from the heavy emotional and mental weight of them. He is a specialist at it! There's no problem too big for Jesus to handle.

All He asks is for you to draw near to Him and put your trust in Him. Get to know Him through His Word and by praying to Him - talk to Him and allow Him the opportunity to reveal Himself to you. Jesus loves you so much, and He is more than able to take care of you if you'll leave those problems in His capable hands.

Too Little Money and Not Enough Bread. Jesus Solves the Problem with a Two-piece Fish Dinner!

Some people think that Jesus only cared about spiritual things, but He was a lot more balanced than that. He cared about people in every way - spirit, soul and body. He taught us that we should live from the heart, serve others and use the wisdom of the Word to live an abundant life.

Jesus was a good preacher. He was anointed, and the Bible tells us in John 7:46 that He spoke like no other man. Jesus told parables (stories) in order to illustrate deep spiritual truths. He also spoke directly about life and issues of the heart. One of the things I really like about Jesus' ministry was that He rarely answered stupid questions! He flat refused to get caught up in legalistic, religious nonsense,

8

and went directly to the source of the problem. Jesus was sincere in His delivery of truth. He also performed miracles, and the more miracles He did, the more the people came out to hear Him preach.

In the Gospel of John chapter six, there is an account of one of Jesus' most famous miracles, and it shows us that He was interested in our physical well-being. He didn't leave us spiritually hungry, and He doesn't want us to be starving physically either! This is a story that will show you what can happen when you decide to leave your problem in the hands of a Specialist.

After these things Jesus went over the sea of Galilee, which is the sea of Tiberias.

And a great multitude followed Him, because they saw His miracles which He did on them that were diseased.

And Jesus went up into a mountain, and there He sat with His disciples.

And the passover, a feast of the Jews, was nigh.

When Jesus then lifted up His eyes, and saw a great company come unto Him, He saith unto Philip, Whence shall we buy bread, that these may eat?

And this He said to prove Him: for He Himself knew what He would do.

John 6:1-6

What I want you to notice is that Jesus didn't ask Philip, "What will YOU do?" He asked Philip, *"Whence shall WE buy bread, that these may eat?"* Jesus included Himself in questioning how they would feed the crowd - this is a very important point.

You see, **God will never ask you to do something that He will not help you to accomplish**. He is with you, and if it is a miracle that is needed, He will be the One to do the miracle - but He will involve you in the process. He may question you with His Word, too. He wants to hear your answer, so that you can find out where your faith is! Your response to His Word should be positive, knowing that He is the One who is able to supply all your needs. He is the Savior. He is the Healer. He is God, and if He asks something of you, He already knows that it's possible for you to accomplish it with His help!

In this instance, Philip didn't really answer the question of "where" they could buy bread. Instead, being the analytical man that he was, Philip began thinking of how much money was in the ministry bag. He looked at the big crowd and tried to figure out just how much it would cost to feed them all.

Philip answered Him, *"Two hundred pennyworth of bread is not sufficient for them, that every one of them may take a little"* (John 6:7).

Then, the other disciples joined in the discussion. John 6:8-9 says, *"One of His disciples, Andrew, Simon Peter's brother, saith unto him, 'There is a lad here, which hath five barley loaves, and two small fishes...'"* Now, that sounds like a great faith statement, doesn't it? Andrew actually looked around to see if there was some food available, but then he blew it and revealed his lack of faith, *"...'but what are they among so many?'"*

Jesus didn't bother getting into the conversation with them. Instead, He decided to show them that God was able to do anything, and since they were thinking entirely outside of faith in God, He didn't bother explaining anything more to them. He just gave them an order, prayed and sprung into action.

And Jesus said, Make the men sit down. Now there was much grass in the place. So the men sat down, in number about five thousand.

And Jesus took the loaves; and when He had given thanks, He distributed to the disciples, and the disciples to them

*that were set down; and likewise of the
fishes as much as they would.*

*When they were filled, He said unto his
disciples. 'Gather up the fragments that
remain, that nothing be lost.'*

*Therefore they that gathered them together,
and filled twelve baskets with the fragments
of the five barley loaves, which remained
over and above unto them that had eaten.*

*Then those men, when they had seen
the miracle that Jesus did, said, This is of
a truth that prophet that should come into
the world.*

John 6:10-14

Notice that Jesus performed the miracle
by first giving thanks to God. Then, He gave
the two-piece fish dinner to His disciples,
and they started giving it to those who were
seated on the grass...all 5,000 of them.

**The miracle happened in the disciples'
hands, not Jesus' hands.** The multiplication
of the loaves and fishes happened as the
disciples were passing the food out. **Yet, it
was God that did the work.** This is another
important point.

God performs the miracles, but He asks us
to get involved in the delivery process. This
is why Jesus valued the laying on of hands.
Mark 16:18 says, *"...they shall lay hands*

12

on the sick, and they shall recover." When we pray for someone and lay our hands on them, it's a point of contact between two human beings who are believing God for a miracle. Matthew 18:19 promises, *"That if two of you shall agree on earth as touching any thing that they shall ask, it shall be done for them of My Father which is in heaven."*

God wants us to be involved in miracles. This involvement not only requires faith but also obedience, which is another point I want to share with you. You see, when Jesus prayed over the meal and passed it to His disciples, it was important that they showed simple faith and obedience to His plan.

Notice that even though the disciples didn't understand how it was going to happen, they did not complain to Jesus about what He asked them to do. Instead, they recognized Him as their leader and simply did what He told them to do. There was no strife, and as a result, 5,000 men and their families were miraculously fed!

Jesus is not surprised by our needs. Why are we surprised by His ability to meet them?

Jesus is never surprised by a need; yet, He seems to surprise everybody with His ability to meet every need!

When you pray about a need that you have, Jesus will never say, "Oh, you've got me on that one! I don't know what to do!" Our Lord is wise and knowing, and we will not be able to surprise Him with our needs, no matter how sudden they seem to come up or how dire they appear to be.

Our human mind tells us that it is only what we can experience with the five senses that matters. We are creatures of habit, and we think in our natural mind that God will only do what has been done in the past. But, God is God! He can make a way where there is no natural way. What He did in biblical times, He can still do today. But, even if He has to do something new to meet your need, He will do it. He's more than able! But, you must be willing to believe it!

Sometimes I wonder why the disciples seemed so surprised by Jesus' actions. After all, Philip knew Jesus personally, and He walked with Him everyday. He witnessed Jesus heal the sick, raise the dead and cast out devils on a regular basis. Yet, when Jesus asked Philip where they could buy bread for the people to eat, immediately Philip looked to the circumstances. Why didn't He immediately speak in faith? Because He forgot that He was talking to The Specialist. He didn't realize yet that, no matter what the situation, Jesus would never be surprised. Instead, He would surprise others with His miracle-working power.

After this miracle, Philip had to work on a defective quality in his character that hindered his ability to respond in faith, his over-analytical mind. You see, Philip had experienced enough with Jesus to know that the natural rules didn't always apply. Jesus healed by doing things in a supernatural way.

When Jesus asked Philip about food, Philip figured it was impossible to feed the 5,000 men and their families. He could have stopped himself after realizing the natural situation and then stirred up his own faith by remembering that Jesus was the Son of God. Instead, he chose to remain analytical, and he let the negative words roll right out of his mouth. Jesus surprised him by making a way where there was no way.

Now, can you imagine what Philip must have been thinking after the miracle was done and he was sent to help gather up the fragments of fish and bread? He must have felt pretty foolish filling up those baskets with the leftovers from a meal that he thought they'd never be able to supply.

You see, all of us have some characteristic that hinders our faith in God.

If you want to know what you need to work on, just listen to what is coming out of your mouth. Luke 6:45 tells us that *out of the abundance of the heart, the mouth speaks.* It's always a good idea to listen to what comes out of your mouth, so that you can spot those weak points and work on ridding yourself of them.

Rid Yourself of Defective Qualities And Depend Upon Your Faith

Andrew also needed to rid himself of the defective qualities of his character that hindered his faith. Just like many people today, Andrew talked out of both sides of his mouth. He started off powerful but blew it before his faith had a chance to start working. It's called being double-minded - and that leads to being "double-mouthed!"

If you have an insurmountable problem, stop worrying about how to work things out in the natural. You can't do the supernatural on your own anyway, so don't allow satan to torment your mind and cripple your faith with fear. Worry can stop your miracle.

Instead, cast all of your cares on The

Specialist, Jesus Christ. I like to say that He has the cure, and He's got the answer. But, in order to receive it, you've got to leave it. You must leave those problems at the foot of the cross and start speaking by faith. James 1:8 tells us, *"A double minded man is unstable in all his ways."* James 4:8 tells us how to get rid of double-mindedness, *"Draw nigh to God, and He will draw nigh to you. Cleanse your hands, ye sinners; and purify your hearts, ye double minded."*

You don't have to try and figure out how to make ends meet. The Bible teaches us that, *"God shall supply all your need according to His riches in glory by Christ Jesus"* (Phil. 4:19). Notice, He said ALL, not just SOME needs. We serve a Master who will never be surprised by our needs. He won't be shocked and unable to come up with an answer for us - **He made us and specializes in helping us**. But, He requires that we go to Him in faith and have patience. Hebrews 6:12 says, *"That ye be not slothful, but followers of them who through faith and patience inherit the promises."*

I have to tell you that I've prayed to God for some phenomenal things, but I've never blown God away with my requests! Sometimes I thought He'd say, "Jesse things are tough up here right now. Gabriel broke his wing last week and Michael is in pretty bad shape himself. We've got some trouble up here." But, He never has told me anything of the sort!

God will never be caught off guard by your prayers, so don't be afraid to rid yourself of the defects that hinder your faith. You can depend upon Him to be faithful to you.

***Never count pennies when
looking at omnipotence.
Until Christ empties your hands,
He can't fill them.***

Why do we count pennies when we serve an omnipotent God? The reason God is unable to bless His people with abundance is because most have their hands gripped on their own meager substance.

We need to realize that until we allow Christ to empty our hands of the meager, He can't fill them with abundance. The boy who gave the fish and the loaves was crucial to the miracle.

Remember, what you have now may not be enough, but if you'll give what you have to The Specialist, He'll multiply it back to you. One day, Jesus will tell you to pick up the fragments, and you'll have baskets overflowing with blessings! So, never count pennies when you are looking at omnipotence. Allow Christ to empty your hands, and He will fill them. This is true for any area of your life.

If you want God to develop a talent in your life, forget about figuring out how you will do it in the natural, and let The Specialist have His way. Remember that your way isn't going to feed or minister to the multitude, but His way will. You must dedicate what you have to Jesus. Allow Him to pray over it, bless it and give it back to you. Only then can He reproduce your talent to such a degree that it will minister to anyone who comes into contact with you.

God is omnipotent, and His ways are always right. His Word will really be like "a lamp unto your feet" if you apply them because He always knows the best way for you to go in life. So, make a decision to live for God all the time, instead of some of the time. Make His Word the last word, and leave your life in the hands of The Specialist. Trust Him to take care of you every step of the way.

Sometimes people want to skirt along the edges of salvation, just close enough to barely slide into Heaven when they die, but this is just not a good way to live. Life is so much better with Jesus all the time instead of just in critical times.

Never get caught in the trap of trying to find scriptures in the Bible that appease your flesh. Don't twist the Word to suit your fleshly desires, but instead, go beyond that type of thinking. Crucify your flesh, and let Christ live through you. Remember, God isn't looking to take what you have; He's looking to give you what He has!

There have been times when I was ministering and I'd think to myself, *God, you have to heal this woman this way.* He'd say, 'No, I'm going to heal her *My* way.' In praying for people, I've had to learn to leave it in the hands of The Specialist. I can't heal anyone. Only Jesus Christ can do the miracle, but I can be a part of it by my obedience. There is no doubt about it. Jesus is the hope of glory, and only He has the title of The Specialist when it comes to healing.

Some people are analytical like Philip, and they want to figure out all the angles, but that's not the best way to live.

When you leave it in the hands of The Specialist, you have to follow His instructions and trust His expertise.

Most of us don't like anyone watching over us while we're working. It is annoying to feel that others don't trust in our ability to do the job. I imagine God must feel the same way when we don't have faith in His ability to take care of our problems.

We must saturate our minds with God's Word so that we'll have faith enough to trust Him with our lives. You know, God sent three million people into a desert, and there wasn't one big corporation out there in need of workers. The Israelites experienced total unemployment. There wasn't a grocery store anywhere that could provide them with food and water. They were following an 80-year-old man into a desert full of nothing but lizards and sand. Yet, God took care of them. He showed Moses and the people the direction they should go and gave them all the food and water they needed.

Moses learned not to count pennies when looking in the face of an omnipotent God. The people were led into the Promised Land because God found a man who loved them enough to take them there.

God seldom uses a person
with a hard or cold heart.
A man must love people
before he can lead them.

If you don't love people, you aren't going to be very successful in the things of God. The same is true within your work life. If you hate what you are doing, then you won't be very productive in it. You must get totally and completely involved in any plan for it to be a success. If you are a carpenter, you have to love building things for people. You must know in your heart that there is nothing you can do better.

People often ask me "Brother Jesse, do you ever get tired of being on the evangelistic field?" I answer, "I sometimes get tired of the traveling, but I never get tired of the field. I love helping people know the Jesus I know." A person must love others, or he will not share the love of Christ with them effectively. You've got to love others in order to save them.

Why did Jesus feed the multitude, heal the sick, raise the dead and cast out devils? He loved people! Not only did He meet their needs, but He also loved them so much that He gave His life for them.

In the reckoning of man, there is a deficit, but in the reckoning of Christ, there is always a surplus.

What the world calls worthless, Christ uses as a vehicle for His servant. One piece of leftover fish or bread was probably worthless in the eyes of many people. But, when you put it all together, it equaled 12 baskets. What everybody else would have ignored, Jesus considered valuable.

When I began in the ministry, I had no help. Everyone thought I was worthless. I even had trouble believing that God could use me.

At first, I really didn't want to go on the evangelistic field. I didn't have the desire. I told God, "Surely, you don't want me. There are a lot of people who want to preach and have the desire, Lord send them. I'll stay home and be a good church member. I'll never miss a service, and I'll give tithes and offerings."

When people heard I was going to preach, I could almost hear them pray, "Surely, you don't want him, God." A preacher told me that things would be tough, and I would starve. "Get ready for it because you will not have many meetings when you first start out," he said. But God proved them all wrong.

In my first year of ministry, I preached 51 revivals, and we only have 52 weeks in a year! I've never called and asked a person for a meeting. Yet, I have thousands of invitations to preach that I can't accept and more coming in just about every day. What has happened? Am I a great man of God? No! What is it? I left this ministry in the hands of The Specialist.

The other day I picked up my first Bible, which is now all tattered and torn. I turned to the first page and read what I'd written down years ago. "I will not book myself, God will book my meetings." God specializes in directing paths and opening doors that we can never open on our own.

People also told me that I would never go on television. Well, God has aired my broadcast in nations all over the world, and He is continuing to open more doors for its airing. My messages are even translated into different languages! People are hearing the Gospel all over the world through the television ministry - and they said it couldn't be done! Jesus said something different!

Jesus said, *"Go ye into all the world, and preach the gospel to every creature"* (Mark 16:15). It was impossible, but *"...they went forth, and preached every where, the Lord working with them, and confirming the word with signs following. Amen"* (Mark 16:20). Jesus did not leave the disciples alone. As they went forth, Jesus, The Specialist, went with them.

As you go into *all the world*, Jesus will always be with you. As you live your life, He is there with you. If you get rid of the defects in your character that hinder your faith in Him, you will no longer be surprised by His hand on your life. His favor, blessing and healing power will become commonplace in your life. As you empty your hands of your meager substance, He will fill them with abundance.

When you love God's people, He can use you to share His message of hope so that they can be saved. Remember, Jesus is real and ready to help you whenever you need it. He's ready to help others too, and He wants to use you to reach those around you. What the world claims is worthless, God can use for His glory. There is *nothing* you cannot do if you leave your life in the hands of The Specialist.

Prayer of Salvation

If you don't know Jesus as your personal Lord and Savior, I'd like to take this opportunity to pray with you. All God asks is for you to come to Him with a sincere heart and accept His plan of salvation through Jesus Christ. Right now, go to Him in prayer. Speak from your heart. The Bible says in Romans 10:9-10 that if you believe on the Lord Jesus Christ with your heart and confess it with your mouth, you will be saved. Your sins will be washed away when you accept what Jesus did for you. Pray this prayer right now:

"Lord Jesus, come into my life. Forgive me of all my sins. I believe that you are the Son of God and that you died on the cross and rose from the dead to make a way for me. Thank you for loving me enough to die for me, for thinking that I was worth it. Today, I accept you into my heart and give myself totally to you. I'm tired of living my own way, and I want to live your way. I need your help. Lord, create a clean heart in me right now and guide me from now on. I love you, Jesus, and I accept you as my Savior. You are now the Lord of my life!"

If you just prayed this prayer, Congratulations!
You're starting a new life! 2 Corinthians 5:17
says when you accept Jesus as your Savior,
*"Old things are passed away; behold, all things
are become new."*

Friend, you have a whole new way of life
to look forward to. You've been given a clean
slate —you are righteous now because of what
Jesus did, and nobody can take that away! You're
saved and starting a brand new life in Christ.

Please write to my ministry and let us know of
your decision so that we can bless you with some
more information and pray for you. God bless
you as you start your new life with God today.

For a free catalog of other books and
audio and visual resources by Jesse Duplantis,
or for information about JDM, call or write:

Jesse Duplantis Ministries
PO Box 1089
Destrehan, LA 70047
985.764.2000
Fax 985.764.0044
or
Visit us online at
www.jdm.org

Look for these other books by
Jesse Duplantis

The Everyday Visionary

The Ministry of Cheerfulness
Also available in Braille

Heaven: Close Encounters of the God Kind
Also available in Braille and Spanish

God Is Not Enough, He's Too Much!
Also available in Braille

Breaking the Power of Natural Law
Also available in Braille

Jambalaya for the Soul
Also available in Braille

Wanting a God You Can Talk To
Also available in Braille

What In Hell Do You Want?

Jesse's Mini-books

Don't Be Affected by the World's Message
The Battle of Life
Running Toward Your Giant
Keep Your Foot on the Devil's Neck
One More Night With the Frogs
The Sovereignty of God
Understanding Salvation
Also available in Spanish

JESSE DUPLANTIS MINISTRIES
Preaching the Gospel to the World